YOUR KNOWLEDGE HAS VALUE

- We will publish your bachelor's and master's thesis, essays and papers

- Your own eBook and book - sold worldwide in all relevant shops

- Earn money with each sale

Upload your text at www.GRIN.com
and publish for free

Bibliographic information published by the German National Library:

The German National Library lists this publication in the National Bibliography; detailed bibliographic data are available on the Internet at http://dnb.dnb.de .

This book is copyright material and must not be copied, reproduced, transferred, distributed, leased, licensed or publicly performed or used in any way except as specifically permitted in writing by the publishers, as allowed under the terms and conditions under which it was purchased or as strictly permitted by applicable copyright law. Any unauthorized distribution or use of this text may be a direct infringement of the author s and publisher s rights and those responsible may be liable in law accordingly.

Imprint:

Copyright © 2010 GRIN Verlag, Open Publishing GmbH
Print and binding: Books on Demand GmbH, Norderstedt Germany
ISBN: 978-3-668-13620-5

This book at GRIN:

http://www.grin.com/en/e-book/159970/the-four-step-decision-making-process-as-a-simple-way-to-arrive-at-rational

Doreen Walter

The Four-Step Decision Making Process as a simple way to arrive at rational decisions

GRIN Publishing

GRIN - Your knowledge has value

Since its foundation in 1998, GRIN has specialized in publishing academic texts by students, college teachers and other academics as e-book and printed book. The website www.grin.com is an ideal platform for presenting term papers, final papers, scientific essays, dissertations and specialist books.

Visit us on the internet:

http://www.grin.com/

http://www.facebook.com/grincom

http://www.twitter.com/grin_com

ESSAY

The Decision Making Process

The Four-Step Decision Making Process is a simple way to arrive at rational decisions. Please illustrate the four steps – in detail and supported by the necessary evidence – using an example from your company!

Sent on: February 08, 2010
Lecturer:
SRH Fernfachhochschule Riedlingen

Subject: Organizational Culture and Change Management
Program of study: Business Administration

By
Doreen Walter

Contents

1 Introduction 4
2 Company Profile   ----   5
3 Four-Step Decision Making Process 5
    3.1 Describing Situation 6
    3.2 Listing Possibilities 6
    3.3 Choosing Selection Criteria 7
    3.4 Acting after Agreement 11
4 Summary 12

Table of figures

Fig. 1: Four-step decision making process..5
Fig. 2: Selection criteria...8
Fig. 3: Relationship outsourcing and core competence-orientation 9
Fig. 4: Selection criteria - evaluation 11

1 Introduction

In the days of globalization, dynamic markets, increasing competition and customers needs making a decision and/or choosing an alternative is becoming progressively more difficult.

Especially in case of complex decisions individuals often think that they cannot cope with it – in spite of their known common sense. Making a decision means balancing multiple objectives and is nearly always accompanied by conditions of uncertainty; uncertainty regarding the future, the consequences of the different alternatives or even due to the variety of goals. But regardless of the respective case to be considered - the more information the "decision makers" have, the better will be the decision.

However, not only the action itself is relevant and decisively – also the selection criteria, which help to orient oneself within the variety of different possibilities and – therefore – guide the decision making. Moreover, particularly these criteria force us to choose not only among the possible courses of action but also among the means of evaluating such actions.

The purpose of the decision making process is to find the best promising of all possible alternatives – subject to the respective goals of the "decision makers".

A successful decision making process should use and pass through some basic steps of decision making. A simple model to follow might be the four-step decision making process that is explained in the following.[1]

This essay is to give an entire overview of the four-step decision making process as the art of balancing different objectives including its single steps. In order to illustrate them, each of those stages is supported by a current example of a decision that is currently to be made at   ----

Based on a short company profile giving some background information regarding the company   ----   , chapter 3 concentrates on the decision making process itself. In the following each of the process steps is theoretically explained and practically accompanied by the mentioned example. The essay ends with a brief conclusion summarizing all results and findings.

---

[1] See Cooke, W. P.: 1985, p. 325f.; Zeleny, M.: 1982, p. XVf.; Drummond, H.: 1991, p. 12; Eisenführ, F./Weber, M.: 1999, p. 1ff.; SRH Riedlingen University: 2008, p. 14f.

2 Company Profile ----

The company was originally founded in ---- by ---- and taken over by today's ---- group in ---- ---- built up several subsidiaries all over the world, e. g. North America, Great Britain, Mexico, Spain, France, China. The company develops, designs, manufactures and supplies powertrain assembly systems including the associated gauging and testing technology for the worldwide automotive manufacturers (OEM[2]) and their sub-contractors. The product range comprises all components for the manual, semi-automatic and automatic assembly of engines/transmissions/ axles, sub-assemblies like cylinder head and steering as well as the entire technology for integrated measurements and the final function test. Today, the parent company in ---- ---- employs approx. 900 own employees and generates a turnover capacity of 150 million Euro (fiscal year 2008/2009).[3]

3 Four-Step Decision Making Process

The four-step decision making process as a unity of different stages is characterized by lots of dynamic interactions and consists of the following interrelated steps:

Fig. 1: Four-step decision making process
(Source: Meridian Group[4])

---

[2] OEM – Original equipment manufacturer
[3] See company profile ---- ---- (January 2010); ---- (03.02.2010), http//:www ----
[4] See Meridian Group (18.12.2009), http//:www.meridiangrp.net

This model contains the essential basics for making decisions – regardless of the respective subject. However, the objectives – and therefore the criteria and the alternatives to be determined – always depend on the individual company-related characteristics (like line of business, size, strategy, products etc.).[5]

3.1 Describing Situation

<u>What are the issues or problems?</u>
First of all it is elementary to get familiar with the exact problem requiring a certain decision. The current situation needs to be described in order to provide as much (reliable!) information as possible to the decision makers.

The international crisis expanding from a financial to a worldwide economic crisis has weakened especially the automotive industry and their suppliers, like ---- . For this reason the ---- group has imposed investment restrictions on all subsidiaries. In order to return to former strength/power several measures have already been taken, e. g. new management board, concepts of lean organization, new project-oriented structure of the entire organization – all supported by an external consulting company.
With regard to these structural changes, the consulting company questions the profitability of the in-house manufacturing. Based on different concepts of the consulting company, the management board now has to decide about the future of the mechanical manufacturing department, which is a strategic decision for or against an outsourcing process.

3.2 Listing Possibilities

<u>What are the possible alternative actions?</u>
The decision makers start searching for alternatives, preferably for those approximating the ideal. The most suitable and best promising alternatives being available and realizable/feasible within the defined schedule of the decision making process are to be discovered. As all alternatives are compared

---
[5] SRH Riedlingen University: 2008, p. 14f.

with the ideal, those which are the farthest away are removed from further consideration.

Beside "available" and "realizable" the word "possibilities" contains another condition – actions can only be serious alternatives, if they are "possible" (in the sense of "allowed" due to potential specifications). The totality of all alternatives is the basic decision makers can choose of.

To avoid going into detail and to simplify the subject regarding all possible options, the following alternatives can be defined for ----

1. Keep the mechanical manufacturing in-house and use the advantage of flexibility and own know-how, examine and improve single processes and create a possible (financing/cooperation) concept to renew the machines in order to be more competitive.

2. Outsource the mechanical manufacturing - incl. employees and entire equipment - to one (preferred solution) or several external companies[6] (depends on the scope potential investors are interested in).

3.3 Choosing Selection Criteria

<u>What is important for the organization?</u>

As already mentioned in the beginning - not only the action and/or alternative itself is relevant but also the selection criteria supporting oneself while asking: How should I/we choose?

By means of those "navigational guidelines"[7] our decisions become more reliable and can be made with greater confidence and understanding.

But not only the action itself is relevant and decisively – also the selection criteria, which help to orient oneself within the variety of different possibilities. Moreover, especially these criteria force us to choose not only among the

---

[6] Hollekamp and Thomsen/Moser distinguish between internal (transfer of products/services to affiliated company, e. g. subsidiary) and external (transfer of processes to legally and economically independent company) outsourcing.
[7] Zeleny, M.: 1982, p. XV

possible numbers of action but also among the means of evaluating such actions.

The following decisive criteria are gradually evaluated:
- *Preservation of competitiveness*
- *Cost reduction impact*
- *Know-how*
- *Risk of capacity utilization*
- *General aspects*

	Criteria	Alternatives	
		in-house mech. manufacturing	external mech. manufacturing
1	preservation of competitiveness	limited competitiveness; high variety of specialized part manufacturer	concentration on core processes (mech. part manufacturing no core competence)
2	cost reduction impact	high - high hourly rates - obsolete machine equipment	to be determined exactly - possibly public (financial) support
3	know-how	high internal know-how	necessity to transfer own know-how
4	risk of capacity utilization	yes	no
5	general aspects		- dependence on suppliers? - resistance of employees? - lack of flexibility? - quite long reaction time for urgent needs

Fig. 2: Selection criteria
(Source: own illustration)

1. Preservation of competitiveness

The high variety of specialized part manufacturers lead to a limited competitiveness and requires a concentration on the custom manufacturing. Due to their higher specialization, many competitors have advantages regarding costs and innovation. Moreover, the mechanical part manufacturing is no core competence of ---- ■ ; outsourcing this department consequently offers the possibility to concentrate on the actual core processes.

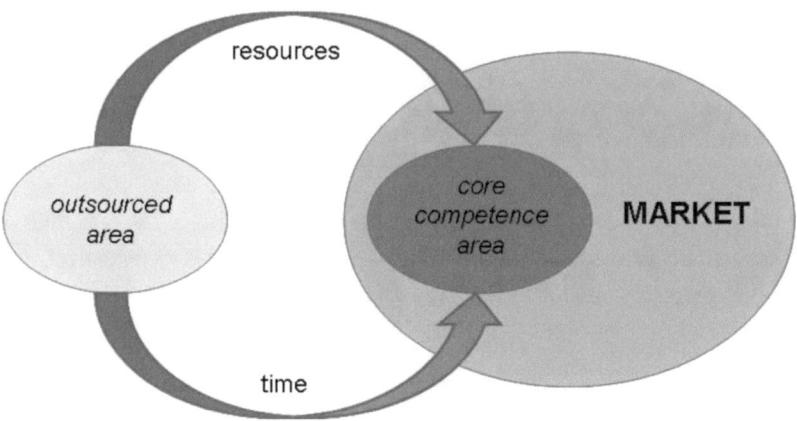

Fig. 3: Relationship outsourcing and core competence-orientation
(Source: taken over - translated - by Thomsen, E.-H./Moser, R.: 2007, p. 30)

2. Cost reduction impact

High hourly rates and obsolete machine equipment that needs to be renewed cause relatively high costs for the mechanical manufacturing. However, due to the current financial situation no further investment is planned. On the other hand, the exact costs in case of an outsourcing of the mechanical manufacturing need to be determined in detail but will probably be less than remaining the department in-house as the fixed cost will just decrease. Studies carried out by market research institutions or consulting companies revealed an estimated cost reduction potential of up to 40% due to outsourcing processes.[8] Furthermore, ---- may possibly expect public (financial) support in case the outsourcing will be realized as cooperation within the region ----.

3. Know-how

Since many years ---- has been a reliable partner in the range of powertrain assembly and has a lot of experience. While the high know-

---

[8] See Hollekamp, M.: 2005, p. 42

how remains internally in case of the in-house mechanical manufacturing, it needs to be transferred to third parties in case of an outsourcing.

4. Risk of capacity utilization

In times of decreasing order situation it is more difficult to keep the approx. 100 employees in the mechanical manufacturing busy than e. g. 20 project engineers of lost orders which are able to support other projects temporarily (or even sales department).

5. General aspects

Outsourcing the mechanical manufacturing may cause various disadvantages. Beside a possible resistance of the employees concerned, a lack of flexibility and a certain dependence on the suppliers may occur as well.

Basically, all criteria focus the return to a profitable business model and an increase of the company value in favor of a long-term existence security, which simultaneously reminds – among other things - on the goals of outsourcing.[9] In the range of plant engineering the core competence consists of engineering services, system integration and commissioning. The benchmark of part costs points out significant cost-saving potentials in case of outsourcing processes. The reference prices are quotation prices of German, Chinese or Slovakian suppliers that have not yet been negotiated finally (!).[10]

Summarizing die findings of all criteria bring out the following results:

---

[9] See Hollekamp, M.: 2005, p. 41ff.
[10] See confidential concept/documents of the external consulting company

Criteria		Alternatives	
		in-house mech. manufacturing	external mech. manufacturing
(1)	preservation of competitiveness	−	+
(2)	cost reduction impact	−	+
(3)	know-how	+	−
(4)	risk of capacity utilization	−	+
(5)	general aspects		−

Fig. 4: Selection criteria - evaluation
(Source: own illustration)

Regarding the final decision, the possibility of the external mechanical manufacturing can be favored meaning an outsourcing of this department.

3.4 Acting after Agreement

<u>Who will do what and when?</u>
Based on the made decision the required tasks need to be defined and assigned to certain offices and/or individuals. It is very important to structure the next steps regarding order and schedule – maybe by a project or team leader – in order to know and be able to check, whether/when/to what extent the responsible offices/individuals get back to the team with any progress.

After the decision has been made in favor of the option "outsource the mechanical manufacturing to one or several external companies", the next steps at ---- need to be defined being coordinated and monitored by a project leader:

- Evaluation of all single outsourcing possibilities and subsequent decision in favor of one outsourcing option (incl. scope) and the respective partners
- Final decision regarding suitable partner (incl. visits of potential partner companies)
- Detailed schedule incl. reorganization towards custom manufacturing
- Compilation of all machines and employees and investment plan for machinery[11]

4 Summary

The previous chapters describe the decision making process as the art of balancing several objectives. Analyzing decisions precisely by means of the four-step decision making process offers the possibility to a decision maker of replacing confusion by clear insight into a desired course of action.

Basically, the four-step decision making process can be described as "work of choosing issues that require attention, setting goals, finding or designing suitable courses of action, and evaluating and choosing among alternative actions."[12] Although the future remains hidden, it is shaped in some way.

However, getting things done and/or making things happen requires a systematic and successful decision making process.

A rational and careful preliminary consideration is of great importance as the process becomes more and more difficult with an increasing number of alternatives.

This process does not serve as an exclusive template how decisions should basically be made. It is rather an approach to support and structure own decision making processes and to make the decision makers more skillful and confident.

---

[11] See confidential concept/documents of the external consulting company
[12] Zey, M.: 1992, p. 32

---- has not invented the outsourcing idea but follows a trend, which came up a few years ago. The last decades can be characterized by an increasing division of labor. Upon the economic globalization, increasing competition and level of technology, the own added value of the companies decreases, while the part of purchased services appropriately increases. Today, outsourcing is increasingly considered as chance to meet the challenges of dynamic markets.

Since the nineties more and more companies concentrate on the strategic aspects of their business activities – their strengths (core competences). Processes beyond those core processes supposed to be outsourcing candidates.[13]

Number of words: 1.948

---

[13] See Specht, D.: 2007, p. 1; Hollekamp, M.: 2005, p. 2ff, 32ff.

References

Company Profile ---- , January 2010

Cooke, W. P. (1985), Quantitative Methods for Management Decisions.

Drummond, H. (1991), Effective Decision Making, London.

Eisenführ, F./Weber, M. (1999), Rationales Entscheiden, Berlin/Heidelberg.

Hollekamp, M. (2005), Strategisches Outsourcing von Geschäftsprozessen, München/Mering.

Meridian Group: The Four-Step Decision Making Process.
URL: http://www.meridiangrp.net/articles/4step.html (18.12.2009)

Specht, D. (2007), Insourcing, Outsourcing, Offshoring, Wiesbaden.

SRH Riedlingen University (2008), Organizational Culture and Change Management, Title No. 0546-02, Riedlingen.

---- . 2007/2008.
URL: http://www. ----

Zeleny, M. (1982), Multiple Criteria Decision Making.

Zey, M. (1992), Decision Making: Alternatives to rational choice models.

YOUR KNOWLEDGE HAS VALUE

- We will publish your bachelor's and master's thesis, essays and papers

- Your own eBook and book - sold worldwide in all relevant shops

- Earn money with each sale

Upload your text at www.GRIN.com
and publish for free